Eros & Psyche
The Eternal Dance of Love And Soul Connections

Eros & Psyche

The Eternal Dance of Love And Soul Connections

Serena Jade

The House of Raising The Sparks, New York

To you, my dear friends

Psyche, my love, we are one, you and me; two supernal energies of the one key. Intuitively, I know we cannot float forever in our heavenly home wrapped in the infinite's light.

Psyche, if we ever become separated from the light and each other, you must trust we will be reunited someday.

When we meet somewhere in time, I will intuitively know you, as you will know me. Our identity of each other is imprinted in the deepest reaches of our soul.

Psyche, do you trust me?

Your deepest most-profound eternal love, Eros

Eros & Psyche: The Eternal Dance of Love and Soul Connections is the first edition published by The House of Raising The Sparks. This book has been available on the market for the past ten years. The feedback has been exceptional, however don't be fooled by the length of this book, putting these concepts into practice is no easy feat. So, when most think of love connections, we don't necessarily think of love for ourselves. *Full acceptance of ourselves is underrated, but absolutely without a doubt the foundation of a healthy relationship.* Full acceptance means knowing yourself and accepting your Body, whole Mind, and Spiritual essence. Soul Mate connections are deeply spiritual, they are making a return to their soul. Twin Flame connections have returned to their soul, and are imbued with charismatic gifts. They reunite after their long devotion to their self. There wouldn't be any point in reuniting, if they did not come home to their own soul, and the infinite.

Soul Mates and Twin Flames are **not** connecting with each other from the traditional way, our society mates. Their connection is from the supernal realm, as above, so below and as below, so above. As such, they must understand themselves, and transform their lower nature to sustain their ethereal connection on earth. These connections are bringing us closer to our own soul, and the Infinite, not away, very important. - Serena Jade, July, 2025

Preface

The ancient story of Eros and Psyche evokes deep purpose within me. In the middle to late centuries of the last millennia, "the eternal lovers" have been depicted in art both in painting and sculpture, by the likes of William Bouguereau, Auguste Rodin, and Antonio Canova to name a few.

The tale of Eros and Psyche stands apart from Cinderella as it explores the spiritual domain. Eros and Psyche symbolize a transcendent love, a sublime union that necessitates comprehension of the eternal soul. This narrative encompasses the soul, soul connections, and a link to Jupiter, reflecting the ancient perception of the supreme deity.

In real life and just like the story of Eros and Psyche, to experience a connection with another person primarily from the soul is connecting with God. From this point forward, when a mystic talks of God, we are seeking the hidden, not discussing a person…we are talking about an unnamable, indescribable light, without qualities, an absolute no-thingness but vast fullness, this light is in time but beyond time, this light is not a form, this light is not finite. And because our focus is within, we lift the veil and touch upon our own soul, which is identical with the unnamable, indescribable light and is without qualities, timeless, formless, and infinite. As the leading scholar of Judaism's Kabbalah, Daniel Matt would say,

"The Big Bang didn't happen somewhere outside of us, no, we began inside the Big Bang, we embody its primordial energy."

Eros and Psyche first meet in the higher dimensions of the supernal world, where they are wrapped in the beloved's energy. But they learn their connection requires an acceptance of self before they are to be reunited on Earth. They must travel into the depths of their ego, and then transform, to be worthy of each other. But not only do they need to be worthy of each other, they must accept their own restrictions.

If the ego can't accept its restrictions, it is in control and not under control. In this instance, the ego cannot serve the soul. And the soul stays bound to the ego, and the cycle goes on. But freedom is accepting and setting your restrictions, right. This is correcting your karma, tikkun. Otherwise, there would be a lot of conflicts, and obstacles preventing soul mates/twin flames from being one with their own self, and each other. Rabbi Berg declares in his book, Wheels of a Soul, "the restrictions placed on us in the present lifetime are in fact, a direct result of mistakes and errors we have made in the past. The past meaning-past lifetimes. To fix and set our tikkun (karma) right, is to bring unity and balance for ourselves, and the universe."

Lucius Apuleius, an adherent of Plato's philosophy and the ancient mystery schools, authored "Eros and Psyche" nearly two millennia ago. Plato distinguished between heavenly love and common love, the former being an immortal bond and the latter a temporal affection.

Apuleius delved into the understanding of the soul's journey to divine union. and to have that reflection mirrored back by spiritual love connections. "Eros and Psyche" symbolize sublime celestial bonds.

The western world fluttered into the dark ages, and the story of Eros and Psyche went into obscurity. The Renaissance lifted the veil and Plato, his students and their knowledge came into light; as a result, five-hundred years later, we can put their wisdom into practice.

Common love is our everyday traditional relationships. The world is made up of relationships based on survival, not connection. One needs to unplug from this unconscious mindset to transcend this mindset! Celestial love would be our modern-day equivalent of a soul mate/twin flame because the soul transcends time and space. We live in a material world; but the soul is intangible. To understand your soul, one must be able to tap into their Spiritual Superpower Point.

Plato knew birth was not the creation of an immortal soul, but a transmigration of a soul from one body to another. Therefore, we cannot make someone a soul mate/twin flame, either we are connected, or we are not.

Not only philosophers but also mystics have taught about the transmigration of the soul, one such teaching is known as gilgul in Judaism.

“Everybody carries the secret trace of the transmigration of his soul in the lineaments of his forehead, and his hands, and in the aura which radiates from his body. And those to whom it is given to decipher this writing of the soul, can aid in its wandering. It is true that this power is acknowledged by Rabbi Cordovero and Rabbi Luria only to the great mystics.”- Major Trends In Jewish Mysticism by Gershom Scholem.

I would like you to grasp, a connection with someone from their immortal soul is not common. But the bond is very possible if we are on a spiritual path, because the path is about returning to your own soul. And the gift for returning to your own soul is the reflection your soul mates/twin flames give to you. So, come along with me, and together let us bring the shadow of our ego, the soul, into the light.

Making A Return To Your Soul

Arise from your slumber! Search your ways and return in *Teshuvah* [to] remember your [soul]!"- Moses Maimonides

Teshuvah means to return. But return where? The Sages have taught over millennia that the essence of each person is his or her soul. The soul is literally a part of G-d on high and is therefore incorruptible and can never truly be blemished by sin. Therefore, when we sin, we are merely losing our way and forgetting who we really are, much like being overtaken by a temporary state of insanity. The journey of *teshuvah* is not about turning over a new leaf or being born again; rather, it is simply finding our way back to the land of our soul. - the Chabad

No individual can ever achieve a completed phase of Teshuvah (A Return), where the individual comes into total control of his fate and destiny, unless he becomes knowledgeable of the unconscious root psychological processes of the soul, along with the knowledge of former lifetimes. - Rabbi Luria-The Gates of Reincarnation

Return To Your Soul והו

For ages you have come and
gone courting this delusion.
For ages you have
run from the pain
and forfeited the ecstasy.

So come, return to
the root of the root
of your own soul.
Although you appear
in earthly form
your essence is
pure Consciousness.

You are the fearless

guardian of Divine Light.
So come, return to
the root of the root
of your own soul.

When you lose
all sense of self
the bonds of a
thousand chains
will vanish.

Lose yourself
completely,
return to
the root of the root
of your own soul.

You descended from Adam,
by the pure Word of God,
but you turned your sight
to the empty show
of this world.

Alas, how can you be
satisfied with so little?
So come, return
to the root of the root
of your own soul.

Why are you so
enchanted by this world
when a mine of gold
lies within you?

Open your eyes
and come ---
Return to
the root of the root
of your own soul.

You were born from
the rays of God's Majesty
when the stars were
in their perfect place.

How long will you
suffer from the blows
of a nonexistent hand?
So come, return
to the root of the root
of your own soul.

You are a ruby
encased in granite.
How long will you
deceive us with
this outer show?

O friend, We can see
the truth in your eyes!
So come, return
to the root of the root
of your own soul.

After one moment with
that glorious Friend
you became loving,
radiant, and ecstatic.

Your eyes were
sweet and full of fire.
Come, return
to the root of the root
of your own soul.

Shams-e Tabriz,
the King of the Tavern
has handed you
an eternal cup,
And God in all
His glory is
pouring the wine.
So come! Drink!

Return
to the root of the root

of your own soul.
Soul of all souls,
life of all life - you are That.

Seen and unseen,
moving and unmoving -
you are That.
The road that leads
to the City is endless;

Go without head and feet
and you'll already be there.
What else could you be? -
You are That.- Rumi

To a Sufi (and all mystics), love is the Lover (the soul) longing to merge with the beloved (the unnamable God). This mystical concept is the foundation for the heart-centered love songs of the 12th and 13th centuries, sung by the Troubadours. This, in turn, set in motion social change in the western part of the world. Love is now an ideal not based on family input but on personal choice, and our collective mindset strives for this love ideal with another person. However, the collective is missing information; a heart-centered connection cannot happen when we are unconsciously seeking someone else to meet our survival needs, and we do not wish to differ from our social circle.

To fulfill our own needs and resurrect our soul to merge with the beloved, takes time and devotion. This is the foundation for a soul connection with another person, and the true eternal definition of soul mates/twin flames touches upon this love. This spiritual love awakens you to balance your own needs and unite with the beloved; we complete us. And now we are whole and complete ourselves, we can reunite with our whole soul in the body of another person.

The Exalted bond between Soul Mates/Twin Flames (Eros) is strongly felt through the sweet whispers of their Soul (Psyche).

The captivating realm of soul mates and twin flames transcend ordinary love and carry a spiritual dimension. Let's explore further:

Soul Mates: These are rare connections where two souls resonate deeply. They share a profound bond, but their encounters are infrequent.

Twin Flames: Even rarer, Twin Flames embody the masculine and feminine polarities of the infinite light. Their souls hold an identical blueprint, originating from a white fiery body. Each Twin Flame is a whole, complete person, destined to be reunited as an androgynous whole.

Non-attachment defines the pinnacle of Soul Mates and Twin Flames. When ego steps aside, the soul prevails.

Remember, these connections are exceptionally rare. Their heightened perception transcends ordinary experiences. In the dance of eternity, Soul Mates and Twin Flames seek each other, somewhere beyond time.

Soul Mates/Twin Flames are supernal connections, that originated in the spiritual realm.

Soul Mates and Twin Flames are connections, a "WOW" to our immortal part of us.

However, our personality has no idea what Soul Mates and Twin Flames are. When we meet a Soul Mate very rare, or Twin Flame extremely rare, our immortal soul recognizes their soul and vice versa. The connection is a deep and profound gift. Soul Mates/ Twin Flames are mates to your Soul.

And a very important, And, to be able to recognize each other, both soul mates and twin flames are awakened at their Super Point. If they are not open at this point, they are not even semi- consciously aware of their own soul, let alone someone else's soul. Authentic Soul Mates and Twin Flames are opened, and the souls involved are tapping into their soul's passion for soul mates, and soul's purpose for twin flames.

The terms Soul Mate/Twin Flame have become our collective ideal, an upgraded version, for a *traditional* temporal social relationship.

However, to partner at a conscious soul level and having that divinity mirored back to you is what these terms imply.

Soul Mates and Twin Flames grow out of a Spiritual quest. Soul Mates and Twin Flames are a mirror of the journey. All parties are deeply spiritual. There wouldn't be any point in reuniting, if they did not come home to their own soul, and the infinite. To partner with a Soul Mate/Twin Flame is to recognize, mirror, and share our Immortal Spiritual essence with each other.

In an ordinary Karmic traditional social relationship, we are connecting to values from our personality. We may come from the same family background and maybe live in the same area. When we form an ordinary relationship, it feels like home, and familiar to our personality, the world is made up of this type of relationship.

Is Your Ego Ready for A Soul Mate/Twin Flame?

Primordial Eros:

"Eros, the god of love, emerged to create the Earth. Before all was silent, bare, and motionless and now all was life, joy and motion."-Early Greek Myth

Christian Mysticism states, Eros appeared and being androgynous, his masculinity is fire from the light, and his femininity, is his soul from the stuff of Pronoia (the universe). All the gods and their angels, when they beheld Eros, became enamored with him. And appearing in all of them, he set them afire: just as from a single lamp, many lamps are lit, and one and the same light is there, but the lamp is not diminished. And the first soul (Psyche) loved Eros…

Eros: The God of love inspires you to listen to your spiritual superpower point and override logic.

Psyche: The Goddess of the soul wants you to understand-the soul is a subtle body existing in the imaginal realm "mediating" …between formless spirit and material substance. - Psychologist, Frances Vaughan

"There is a voice that doesn't use words. Listen." -Rumi

"Words are a pretext. It is the inner bond that draws one person to another, not words."- Rumi

Wrapped in light, young Eros, the true spiritual connection that binds soul mates/twin flames together, gives Psyche, who represents our soul, a kiss. This painted vision suggests the soul's home is in the supernal world. We first meet our spiritual mates in our eternal residence. At the deepest level, our identity is imprinted on each other forever.

Raise Your Hands To The Supernal World And Pray, That We Will Be Reunited With Our Eternal Mates One Day

Meeting our eternal mates is like reuniting with old friends. However, our soul has accumulated unhealthy situations, and influences our personality flaws. Any negativity needs to be worked out within, so it does take some praying that we will be reunited. We do not pray that we are going to be reunited, and now we live happily ever after. We pray and work on making our personality whole. Then all the forces of the universe will bring our souls together again; reunited whole and complete, a true partnership.

All religions have a hidden mystical understanding. Judaism has the Kabbalah, Christianity has Gnosticism, Islam has Sufism, Hinduism has Tantra. Buddhism, Jainism, Taoism and Confucianism are derived from Tantra. The mainstream of religion is the literal basic understanding, but their esoteric counterparts go deeper beyond the surface and are embedded in their traditions. All esoteric wisdom is very similar as they focus on the soul within the person, and a God who cannot be named. When someone embarks on the esoteric path, they are mystics. **This is not about belief, but about self-knowledge.**

Mysticism originates from the Greek word for 'that which is hidden.' Typically, mystical experiences are silent and beyond understanding. It involves closing one's eyes to the physical world while opening the 'third eye,' and remaining silent to immerse oneself in the spiritual enigma both within and around us.

The Beloved of the Soul: Compassionate one draw your servant to your will. Then your servant will hurry like a hart to bow before your majesty. To him, your friendship will be sweeter than the dripping of the honeycomb and all the taste.

Majestic, beautiful, radiance of the universe, my soul is sick for your love. Please G-d, heal her now by showing her the pleasantness of your radiance. Then she will be strengthened and healed and eternal gladness will be hers.

What Early Jewish Mysticism teaches us about modern day terms such as: Soul Mates and Twin Flames...

Mystic rabbis understood initiated knowledge and described creation as worlds forming and annihilating from the great hidden God (the infinite, the beloved). Very much like what we now know today as the creation of the Big Bang, particles of energy forming and annihilating. As time moved on, the universe formed seven groups of souls with leaders and followers but as a result were separated from their original nature.

Samael was a leader of one of the groups, but he was labeled evil. He was labeled evil not because of his nature, but because of his desire to unite and intimately mingle with an emanation before the separation of his original nature. In the *Treatise on the Left Emanation,* Lilith is the Twin Soul to Samael. Lilith and Samael were born in a spiritual birth as one twin like forms. Both had emanated from the energy of all energies.

Rabbi Issac Luria refers to the relationship between certain souls in accordance with the place which they originally occupied in the supernal world. There are relationships between souls and even families of souls, which somehow constitute a dynamic whole and react upon one another. -Gate of Reincarnations -

These souls have a special aptitude for assisting each other and supplementing each other's actions and can also by their piety lift up those members of their group who have fallen onto a lower plane and can enable them to start on the return journey to higher forms of existence. — Gershom Scholem- scholar of Jewish Mysticism

The Zohar clearly states, "Note that all the figures of souls that are to be born stand before the almighty in pairs. Souls are divided into male and female and after they worked their way through the corridors of reincarnation and have gained correction (karma), sufficient to merit one another, the almighty brings them back together. There is no bliss in the physical universe greater than that of reunification. But it must be earned by soul growth over many lifetimes." -Rabbi Berg

Plato stated ..."If we conduct ourselves with reverence towards the gods, then the gods will restore us to our original nature, healed and blessed with perfect happiness."-Excerpt from Plato's Symposium

Ancient wisdom clearly states, to return to our original nature, we must set our restrictions right and return to the source of our supernal nature. But our soul has forgotten that we were once whole, and the quest to become one again, has a lot of detours.

Ancient Greek Wisdom: Know Thyself!

To be self-knowledgeable is to be psychologically disciplined and reflective. When we acquire psychological wisdom, we can start to understand our supernal nature. However, it takes time and a willingness to want to be a whole person, and have healthy relationships, first with the self, and then with others!

"A commitment to self -knowledge and self-improvement is the first requirement of any individual who wishes to take control of his life and alter his destiny if necessary. Once that commitment is made, results can be immediate and fulfilling. Not only will we be happier in the quest to elevate our soul, but also, we shall find that pursuit of this goal begins to alleviate a great deal of the suffering initially dictated by our Tikkun (Karma) pattern." -Rabbi Berg.

The purpose of psychoanalysis is to dive into the unconscious. A good therapist will help the patient make their unconscious, conscious. However, as a society we are so consumed with taking a drug, rather than uncovering our unconscious. Just like the line from the Netflix series Gypsy, there is one force more powerful than free will...our unconscious. It doesn't matter if we take a pill or not, our unconscious is always there directing our lives, whether we like it or not.

"Consequently, the crystal-clear message appears to be that fate, destiny, decisions, and human behavior cannot be understood without taking the unconscious psychological process into account."-Rabbi Berg-To The Power of One

"Until we make the unconscious, conscious it will direct our lives and we will call it fate."-Carl Jung

"To seek myself and know who I was and who in what manner, I now am that I may again know that which I was."- Gnostic wisdom.

I Am That Which Was, Is And Ever Shall Be, A Jewel In The Crown of The Divine Self, A Star In The Firmament of The Luminous One. -Rumi

Hippolytus was an early Christian leader and had contact with the Gnostics. Hippolytus hinted that the Gnostics were psychologists, but obviously were not identified as such. Hippolytus has stated that the Christian mystics referred to as Gnostics said, "It is their understanding that the soul is extremely hard to find and difficult to comprehend, and that knowledge of the whole self is just as difficult. But for a person to know thyself is to know God."

"The dream is the small hidden door in the deepest and most intimate sanctum of the soul, which opens to that primeval cosmic night that was soul long before there was conscious ego and will be soul far beyond what a conscious ego could ever reach.-Part of the human Self or Soul is not subject to laws of space and time."-Carl Jung

~ Carl Jung

Let your mind go into the spiritual realm, and picture groups of energy forming and disappearing, and then forming again but separated from their main source. The cosmic energy of your soul, separated from its main source, formed these groups, and then the whole soul separated from the group, and then from each other.

This paragraph is taken from a great book titled, Twin Souls: A Guide to Finding Your True Spiritual Partner: "The groups separate into ever smaller units. As the groups separate, each of them is endowed with its own characteristics. The smaller the groups, the more closely the souls within them cohere. They memorize one another, the longer the association, the more indelible will be the memory. By this memory they will find their way back to one another in the time of ascent."

Dr. Brian Weiss, the author of the best-selling book, Many Lives, Many Masters, has a fabulous description on soul groups...

I like to think of soul relationships as similar to a large tree with a thousand leaves on it. Those leaves that are on your twig are intimately close to you. You may even share experiences, among yourselves. There may be three or four or five leaves on your twig.

You are also highly and closely related to the leaves on the branch next to yours. They share a common limb. They are close to you, but not as close as the leaves on your own twig.

As you extend farther out along the tree, you are still related to these other souls, but not as closely as those in your immediate proximity. You are all part of one tree and one trunk. You share experiences. You know each other. But those on your twig are the closest.

I would like to add the closest is the leaf itself, and that whole soul is your soul's counterpart-your twin flame.

Soul Mates/Twin Flames "see" one another at the level of the soul. Knowing the difference between the ego (personality) and soul is paramount for an authentic soul mate experience.

Did you ever stop to wonder: is your personality all there is of you? Do you ever wonder about the soul?

If there isn't any separation, one thinks the Ego is the Soul. There must be separation before there is unity.

First, Our Personality

When we are young, we are told what is acceptable, so we repress the exact opposite, and hence, we have created our personality.

Through the ego, our personality develops, which acts as a stabilizer for us. We can communicate verbally with our personality. Its highest function is that of reasoning and to be able to live in the world.

The ego does everything in its power to stay safe and secure, becoming identified with our opposites is not easy. That is why becoming whole is a Hero/Heroine's journey.

Soul mates/twin flames complete us at the soul level and not the ego. Collectively, we want the other person to complete us. But no one can complete us because it is our job to make our personality whole.

The material world is valued by our personality and is perceived by the five senses. This is defined in what we do in the world, not who we really are on the inside. All of us are taught only to see the personality and nothing else. As we live our life, we try to fit in with our family and with society, and we end up adopting certain behaviors. Deeply ingrained patterns of thought will tell us how we will act or react under different situations.

This conduct gets ingrained within our personality each year we live.

Our personality follows the acceptable worldview of our family and public. What we can outwardly see, touch, taste, smell and hear dominates. Our personality is a valuable asset we have, as it grants us is the ability to live in our world. However, if we are only identified with the ego, this conscious mind conceals the deeper mysteries from us. As Rumi would say, "The ego is a veil between humans and God."

Now for the Soul

The deepest most reaches of our inner being. It is a form of consciousness permeated in and around us, transcending time, and space. The soul does not take on a form like our personality does, but instead is more abstract. It is not material therefore we cannot perceive it with our five senses. The soul is ruled by our *inner* world, instead of our *outer* world. The five senses do not have any power in this inner world, so we must tap into another sense. What we see, hear and sense inwardly is our soul speaking to us. The soul is the source through which spiritual energy can reach us. All matter possesses a soul but not everyone expresses their spiritual nature.

An imaginary, enigmatic veil covers your personality, and once lifted the spark of the Divine is witnessed in all its intoxicating joy. The piercing vibration of our eternal existence makes us scream with delight. We need to feel this connection as it is not seen with the two regular eyes. It is an intuitive sensing felt within us and around us. We arise from unawareness and realize our supernal self. There is an overwhelming happiness knowing that the most cherished place inside of you is connected with an invincible exalted force outside of you.

To put it simply, our personality is a human structure, and our *soul* is a spiritual construct. Our personality's thoughts bombard us most of our lives, and yet silence is the key to discovering your soul. The soul is trapped by the personality, and if you ignore it, you are dishonoring your radiant gem. Why would someone not listen to his or her soul? The answer is that the soul's voice is an inner authority, as opposed to an outer authority that adheres to the rules of our social order.

"I've been a seeker and I still am, but I stopped asking the books and the stars. [The tarot card readers, energy workers, psychics, spirit guides.]
I started listening to the teaching of my soul."-
Rumi

Genuine security comes when you own all the opposites of your personality. You can now truly listen to your soul and celebrate why your eternal being is here on Earth. We begin to know we are more than our rational mind, and the depth of our inner being will be wrapped in joyfulness. We can understand the connection deep within, as we know our soul is one with the universe.

The more conscious we become we begin, to be inquisitive about the science of physics, and the world's religions. As we begin to understand the science of physics, plus all the earth's religions; then we can absorb the universal wisdom underneath all religions.

Religion means to unite us back to our divine origin, and science gives us physical evidence of our origin. This is what all religions on the deepest level are supposed to do: Bring us back to ourselves and this in turn will bring us back to humanity!

The personality is a human structure and must shift to a higher feeling of self-worth; and it is only then that the personality can believe, think, and act on what the soul is saying.

The soul is a spiritual construct, but your personality could have an obligation to a particular religion. To be truly spiritual is to have a commitment to your soul.

Connecting your human identity with your supernal nature is a fabulous arrangement for you and the world!

A Rabbi Talking…

"When we achieve a spiritual awakening, we become aware of our ego as a significant obstacle in our ascent. The soul's enslavement to the ego is the most difficult and burdensome thing for it to overcome on its upward journey. A significant step on every path to the soul, then, is the intellectual and emotional effort we give to limiting the power of the ego. This enterprise is known as "self-nullification," and it is at the core of our spiritual striving. It does not involve minimizing our identity to become nothing; rather, it is a process that is meant to limit the control of the ego. Setting limits and boundaries for the ego so that it does not turn our soul into a tool in service of a foreign god is therefore a fundamental task for us all." -Rabbi Steinsaltz

I hope you have a better understanding of the difference between the personality and the soul.

Our collective values regarding relationships originated a long time ago. The traditional values such as mating to fit in with our family and friends need to change, if we want to connect on a deeper level. The old values have extraordinarily little awareness of the soul. I encourage you to reach for a relationship that is grounded on this earth, but the essence of the connection is made in heaven-better known as soul mates/twin flames.

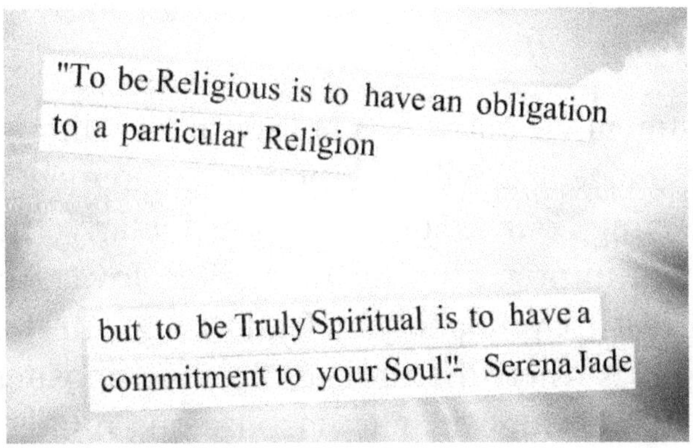
"To be Religious is to have an obligation
to a particular Religion
but to be Truly Spiritual is to have a
commitment to your Soul."- Serena Jade

Eros and Psyche are connected by the exalted love of their soul. However, their personalities are imbued with self-loathing. If you have a desire to mate at an exceedingly high spiritual level, your personality must be up to par with your everlasting being.

Years ago, I met a woman who was a psychotherapist. One day we are talking, I am telling her about my life, and she says I should seek a therapist. Then Lorelle says something very profound: ***Psychotherapy is like making a study of yourself.***

The investment we make psychologically will improve our self/body-image and will also prepare us to meet our own soul. Meeting our soul is a particularly important achievement in preparing for an exalted love. According to the great psychoanalyst Carl Jung, the personal unconscious is where the ego's repressed opposites live. If we travel far enough in our unconscious mind, we will uncover our opposites, and touch upon the sensation and memories of our soul.

Are you ready to touch your opposites and the supernal mystery within you?

Authentic soul mates/twin flames wake up and realize the higher dimensions in the other-true Soul Mates/twin flames!

"The key to [spiritual] growth is the introduction of higher dimensions of consciousness into our awareness."- Lao Tzu.

Spiritual growth is the introduction of higher consciousness. Spiritual growth is NOT the same as personal growth. Personal growth relates to our ego and spiritual growth relates to our soul. When we live from the heart, we balance our ego and soul in the here and now. In an ordinary relationship, we are attracted to someone for two reasons ...We are sexually attracted to their appearance, and their values.

More importantly, they also have the missing personality traits we need to be whole. When we get involved in this relationship it feels wonderful in the beginning. Plato understood this phenomenon and said 2500 years ago, "Love is just a name we give to the desire and pursuit of wholeness." We feel elated and euphoric, however, this sense of enlightenment does not last for long.

Why do you think this is? The other person is temporarily making you feel whole. But this is a false sense of wholeness. After the initial phase both people start to create power struggles with the missing traits, and the soul rarely comes in the picture…

Psyche Speaks Her Truth…

I am Psyche and my name means "Soul" in Greek. The deep mystery of our immortal essence is unconscious to most people. Therefore, what is unconscious is considered dark and evil, images like witches, warlocks, sorcery, and vampires come to mind when we think of an otherworldly realm.

I would like you to know, our souls are here to be rediscovered. Direct contact with the soul transcends our ordinary mind and creates a sacred relationship within. However, the ego and soul do not achieve an equal balance on their own. One will take over the other, until we live from the heart and create our whole self.

My counterpart, Eros, is the exalted bond between your soul and your soul's mates and God.

When your conscious mind has a strong foundation and becomes content, owns its power and has the ability to express your true voice, you become autonomous. You are now ready to journey onto the bridge that connects your ego with your soul.

Conquer the fear of abandonment or engulfment, balance your heart to emotionally give and receive, and let your ego join your soul.

When you are ready to cross the bridge, you will enter the realm of my domain. With practice and determination, your ego mind and soul will be together as one. However, we need to look within and discover issues we do not want to know about.

You might answer, "I don't want to."

If you do not look within, you will never have peace and never know your soul. Transform your ego into wholeness, and your heart is there to help you create harmony.

When you are in touch with your emotions of fear, guilt and shame, your ego and heart will be working together as a team. You will have the power within to make wise choices in life. You will also be accepting of your uniqueness, and your ego will be efficient to serve your soul!

Isn't that great?

You might answer, “Yes, it is, but why can’t I stay in the moment? I don’t want to open a can of worms and relive events and emotions that are no longer relevant to my present state.”

Do you want peace and love? Do you want to know the purpose of your life? Do you want to know what happens after you die? Do you want to meet your soul mates/twin flame? Do you want to find a deeper meaning to your life?

You might answer, “Yes I do.”

You can only have peace and live the purpose of your life when your ego joins your soul. You can only meet and join Eros-an exalted bond, only if you connect your ego with your soul.

You might answer, “I want to know my soul; I want to balance my heart.”

Unblock the emotions that lay dormant within you and release the hurt that you experienced from your past. Release the anger and frustration that is keeping you in a prison. Become vulnerable with safe people you can trust and will not judge you.

Let go of your co-dependent ways in which you relate to another. Stop taking care of other people’s needs and they will halt being dependent on you. Stop being dependent and take care of your own needs; become secure so you can function on your own. Then you will be free to create a life, full of love and peace within and without.

You might answer, “But how do I do it?”

Get the needs of your ego balanced, so you will be secure. You will release your blocked emotions, and your heart will be balanced, so you can serve your soul …

Many years later, you say, “I did it, after many long arduous years I journeyed to that place within myself. I created a strong foundation; I am content, I own my personal power and I am autonomous. I transformed all my deep wounds and I am here on the bridge. I am now crossing the bridge and entering the realm of my soul- Psyche as it is called in Greek!”

The Age of Aquarius is the age of Spirit, uniting our human (ego) with our spiritual (soul). -"Moses said, "I will not give up until I reach the point where the two seas meet, though I spend years and years in travel." -The Holy Qur'an- Sufi Mystics (and all mystics) teach, Where the two seas meet is the Mystical Marriage (Unio Mystica) of our Human identity and Spiritual Nature- To fully incarnate the Soul into Human Destiny-we live from the Heart, the bridge the connects the Human to the Spiritual.

The Mystical Marriage (Unio Mystica) comes when the ego is under control, not in control- then the union of ego and soul are walking together hand in hand; wrapping them with its encircling light, the Infinite shines within them, and all around them.

I encourage each one of you; create a strong foundation, you are responsible for you, own your space and power, strive to be autonomous and speak your truth. Cross the bridge that connects your lower identity with your higher nature. Live life, your life from your heart!

Lucius Apuleius wrote the beautiful allegory of *Eros and Psyche* around nineteen-hundred years ago. Mr. Apuleius lived when Rome ruled the world and was a follower of Plato. He was an initiate of the sacred religion of Greco-Roman society. Therefore, he was well-versed in the deep mystery of the soul.

One sultry night in ancient Greece, Socrates and five other philosophers join, and the *Symposium* is created. Plato, a student of Socrates, writes down the dialogue in which these enormous thinkers are engaged. This great literary work about love has survived the ages. These amazing men of thought gave us wisdom about two types of love: common love and celestial love.

To understand common love is amazingly simple: it is found in our everyday relationships. Celestial love is an extraordinary bond, the aim of which is to connect our gift from the Divine with another person.

We have many soul mates on our branch and twig, but our twin soul is the ultimate soul mate.

THE ULTIMATE SOUL MATE IS
YOUR DEEPEST ETERNAL LOVE!-
AUTHOR SERENA JADE

Eros and Psyche represent the ultimate. The knowledge that each one of us has a true other half is not new. Ancient philosophers and members of the esoteric clergy have been talking about our twin for thousands of years. Many moons ago, Plato studied in Heliopolis, Egypt. Heliopolis was a place to learn the deeper mysteries of life. Living in Heliopolis, one could not help, but hear the creation story of Atum…

In the beginning, there was darkness and Atum. Atum contained both male and female within. Atum manifested Shu, the god of air and Tefnut, the goddess of moisture. It is said, Shu and Tefnut possessed one soul between them!

In Ancient Greece, the creation story went like this…In the beginning there was darkness and Nyx. Nyx laid an egg, and after many years, suddenly Eros rose out of the shell. Eros, the God of love, manifested the male and female within himself, and created Mother Earth and Father Sky.

Modern Day Wisdom is Ancient…

In a galaxy far far away...one tiny Atom, collides with another universe and our universe is in motion. Our solar system, our energy and our Earth have been morphing for 14-billion years!

The hidden wisdom of Judaism said 500 years ago, "When the contracted into itself, separating itself from the Vessel, the Vessel shattered, giving birth to the universe as we know it. This is known in Kabbalah as *shvirat ha'kelim*, or the Shattering of the Vessels. And it is that moment, that is known as the Big Bang; Kabbalists call it *Tzimtzum*.

When the Holy One created man, the Nameless force made man of the upper and lower, of the angelic and of the human. Man was created male/female, then separated.

The Cosmology of The Gnostics:

When mystics want to explain the universe, they use everyday language, but they transcend their command of language by putting forth knowledge from the understanding of the supernal world, not by this third dimensional world, as such: "The father was surrounded by luminous spiritual water. He gazed into the water and saw his reflection and became the mother, his female counterpart. She gave birth to a spark of light. From the son came four luminary rulers, from the rulers we generate Sophia, the wisdom of the light. But Sophia drank the waters of forgetfulness and lost the gnosis (knowledge). But the capacity to revive gnosis lies dormant within, Sophia. All is needed is a Christ, a savior to reveal the gnosis to her." -Secret Book of John

.

The Gnostic Jesus Christ was the spark of light, who was the offspring of the Father, Mother God. Hence, I am the light before all things, that is a primordial light. Gnostic Jesus Christ was not a deity who was worshipped as a God, but a teacher who liberated one's soul from ignorance of forgetfulness.

Every particle Out of the original unity of being there is a fragmentation and dispersal of beings, the last stage being the splitting of one soul into two. – The Sufis by Idries Shah

From one tiny Atom, physicists know bundles of particles and anti-particles manifested out of brilliant energy. The particles of energy are always produced as a pair. Particles created out of the Big Bang appears to have a partner particle. Physicists right now only see matter. However, they understand the universe produces about as much matter as antimatter. Physicists know matter and antimatter, their "Twin" particle would be just like, their mirror image.

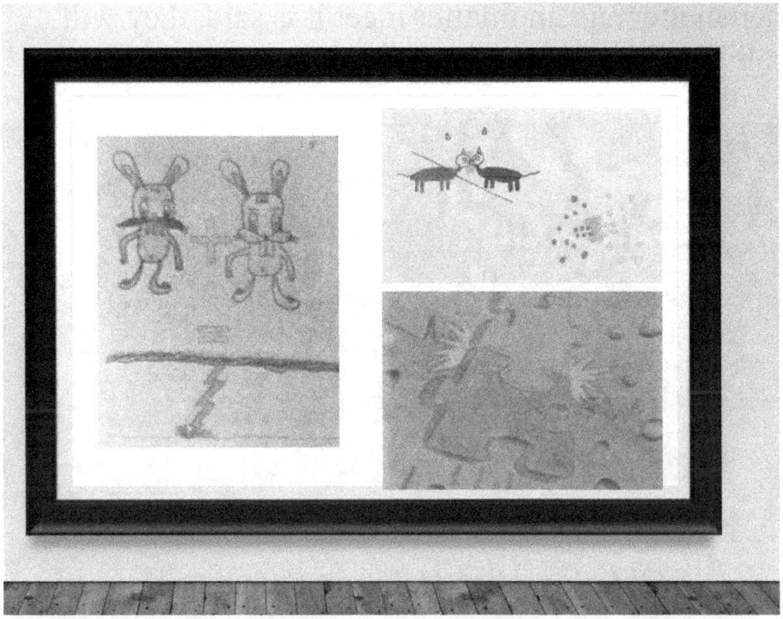

Children’s drawings of matter and antimatter from CERN When matter and antimatter meet, a third entity is present, energy! - The *Infinite, Beloved!*

Did you know the ancient Greeks knew of the Atom, but they could not prove it?

The matter and antimatter story could certainly mirror the creation stories of yesterday and Plato's understanding; “It was their very essence that had been split in two, so each half missed its other half.”- Excerpt from Symposium.

When matter and antimatter meet it is said, they will annihilate or there will be an explosion of joy?

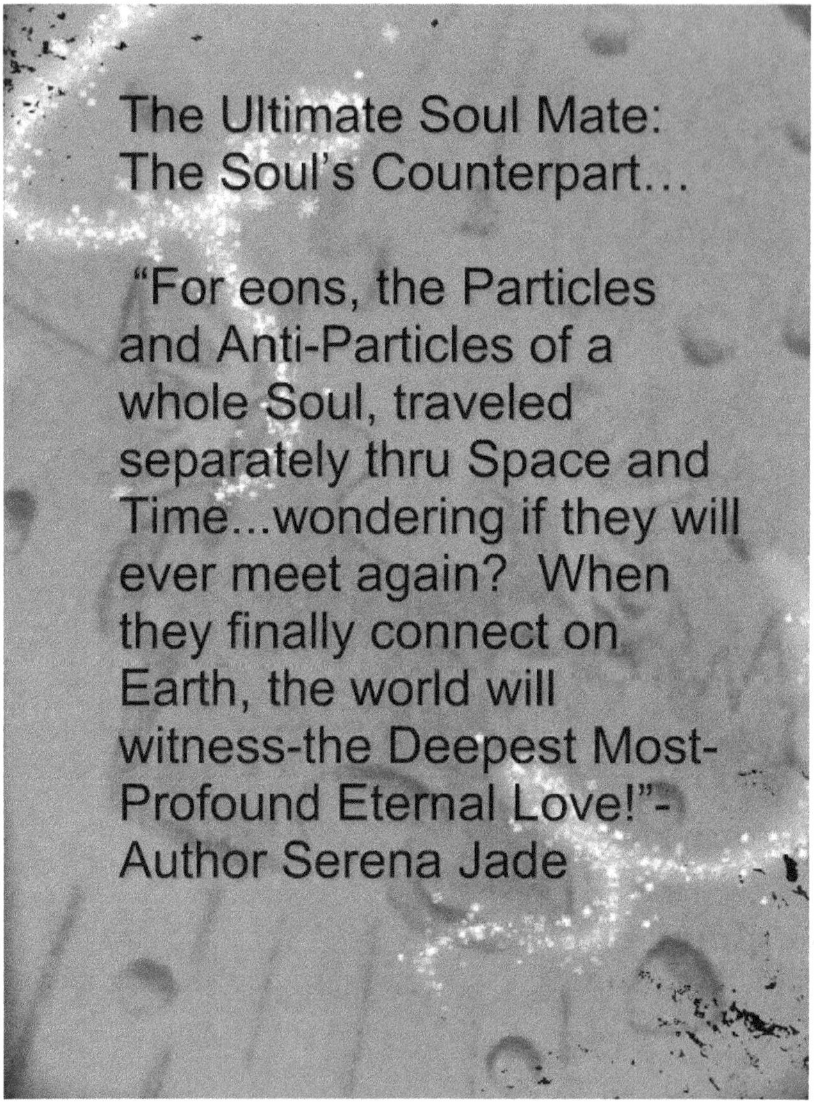

Which do you want annihilation or joy?

Do you choose joy?

Do you have the self-discipline to make your personality whole, and not fall into the allure of the marriage mystique?

This means you must be alone for years; are you willing to be alone?

We are living in a society that can absorb the knowledge about our twin and connect at a deep level. We have the freedom in the west to live on our own first and become whole without the added pressure to marry. However, we must listen within and know that this relationship is possible. So, that we do not succumb to the pressures of our family and friends.

Are you willing to know yourself so that you will be ready for your twin?

Your personality finally makes the union with your soul and brings together your human nature with your spiritual essence-YOU COMPLETE YOU!

The Twin Soul Model

Two separate complete individuals, mirroring their Divine Supernal qualities, and becoming greater and stronger together!

Mr. Apuleius takes the wisdom of Plato and writes the story of Cupid and Psyche; aka Eros and Psyche in the middle of his book, *The Golden Ass,* originally known as *The Metamorphoses of Apuleius.* It is the only Latin piece of literature to survive in its entirety. *The Golden Ass* is written in Latin, but Mr. Apuleius apologizes for it should have been written in Greek. The book is about Mr. Apuleius travels and interest in magic which brings about his transformations.

Eros and Psyche are symbols: Psyche represents the soul and Eros, a soul connection. Psyche (regardless of gender) must travel into the depths of the mind to be worthy of profound love.

The Golden Ass is written in Latin, so Mr. Apuleius uses the Roman version of the Gods and Goddesses. Our western world is familiar with the Roman Goddess of Love-Venus as opposed to the Greek-Aphrodite, and the Roman God of Love- Cupid instead of the Greek–Eros.

However, Eros and Cupid are worlds apart and to reach Eros is an extremely high aim, for it is an exalted bond.

Eros is the lover, the god who mediates between matter and spirit.

Carl Jung was right on target when he talked about Eros…

Eros belongs on one side to man's primordial animal nature, which will endure as long as man has an animal body. On the other side, he is related to the highest forms of the spirit. But he thrives only when spirit and instinct are in right harmony.

Carl Jung was influenced by Plato's Symposium. In Symposium, Diotima, the prophet/ priestess teaches Socrates about Eros…

Eros occupies the middle ground, Diotima replied. Eros is an important spirit. All spirits occupy the middle ground between mortality and immortality. As mediators between the two, they fill the remaining space, and so make the universe an interconnected whole. Mortality and immortality cannot meet directly unless, the gods communicate and converse with humans in their sleep or when conscious by means of spirits. Skill in this area is what makes a person spiritual, whereas skill in any other art or craft ties a person to the material world.

The famous psychic Edgar Cayce agrees, soul mates/twin flames are regular relationships between people who possess an extraordinary connection. Mr. Cayce goes on to say the story of soul mates/twin flames is really the story of spiritual awakening. For this reason, ultimately our search for soul mates/twin flames is really a search for God.

Cupid is an actor of love…

The word cupid is from the Latin root meaning (desire). Desire is a misleading word because the meaning is one of emotional attachment. When we have attachments, we want to control the situation. When we want control, our soul is not at work, our egos are.

To have power over your mind and emotions is authentic and you are worthy of all good things. Your mind and emotions are working as a team. In your mind's eye, you are envisioning abundance and are looking forward to watching the overflowing of riches manifest. You are at a place of no doubt!

To desire is a desperate yearning, wanting, a despair that if you do not have such and such, you feel like you are not going to survive. You are full of doubt and unworthiness, your mind and emotions are not on the same team.

A non-attached mind is clear, and an attached mind **desires** a certain result, but **fears** the result will not be obtained. Clearly attachment is full of doubt and non-attachment exudes confidence. So, a nonattached mind is alive, and the wicked emotions of fear, guilt, and shame are transformed. One knows they are worthy, and there is not any lack, which would equal the ultimate-this is the law of Attraction!

The Goddess of Love is forming out of a shell in the middle of the sea, just off the island of Cyprus.

Gods and Goddesses of the ocean are welcoming Aphrodite onto the earth. Poseidon's tritons are blowing charismatic music into the air, creating a sound the world will know as love. Aphrodite is unashamed of her body. She exudes sensuality and is welcomed by angels who want to show her and the world that true love is within our reach.

Heavenly Love and Common Love

"As we all know, love and Aphrodite are inseparable. The duality of Aphrodite is undeniable: One Aphrodite, the one we call celestial, is older. The other, the younger one is called common." –Plato

Socrates was most concerned with celestial love, because not only was it important for this life, but the life that comes after this one as well; the discovery of our immortality is very virtuous. In other words, the bond between celestial soul mates/twin flames is an infinite connection, as opposed to the self-interests between personalities.

The common traditional karmic love has to do with our personality and survival needs. Celestial love connects us with our soul mates; linking us with each other's immortal soul. The common karmic relationship will just satisfy our survival needs, karmic obstacles will infuse chaos, and the soul is unconscious to the parties involved.

Celestial love is the key that unlocks the door to immortal love. She is a symbol for us to uncover deep wounded issues that are holding us back to connect with eternal love. She leads us to feel emotions that are so repressed, so we can transform and live our potential.

Celestial Aphrodite pushes you to journey deep within. She will coax you to discover your own soul and prove to yourself that you are worthy of an exalted bond.

She leads us to reach for the ultimate… non-attachment. A security within and not from the other person has been achieved after many long arduous years.

Are you ready for celestial love?

If so, are you ready to journey into your own depths?

“The descent into the depths will bring healing.”-Carl Jung.

The soul mate/ twin flame extraordinary encounter makes one feel as if they just arrived at a temple. They have been given access to the Divine, as they enter the room where the holy of holies resides, they can sense the spark of the almighty deep within each other.

In the Age of Aries, only the high priest had access to the inner sanctum of the Temple, the holy of holies, where the almighty dwelled. In the Age of Aquarius, we are the high Priest/Priestess, we have access to the direct inner sanctum of our soul, and the soul of another. When we touch the inner sanctum, we step on holy ground.

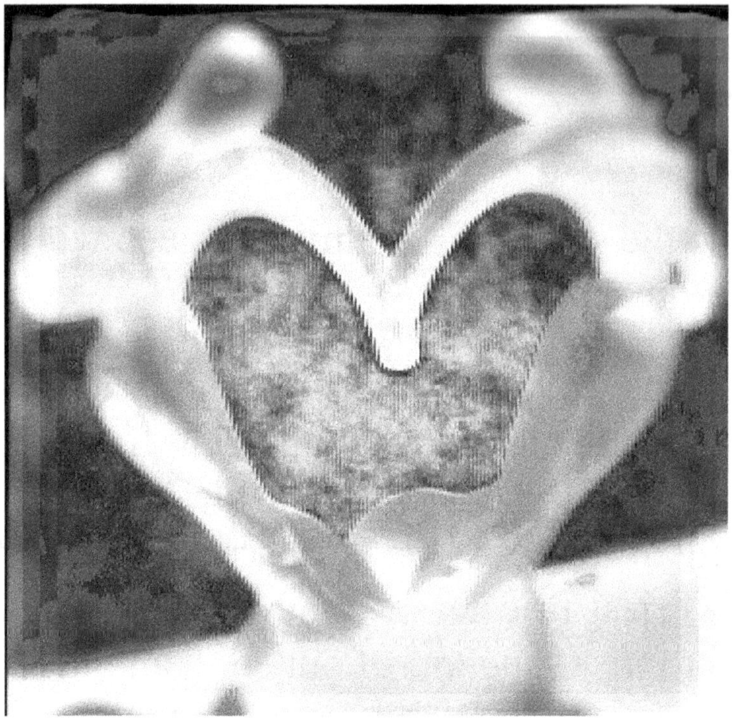

“The minute I heard my first love story, I started looking for you, not knowing how blind that was. [True] lovers don’t finally meet somewhere, they’re in each other all along.”-Rumi.

The Soul is ineffable; therefore, true soul mates/twin flames are indescribably connected.

The story of Eros and Psyche

The King and Queen of a distant, exotic realm have three daughters, with the beautiful Psyche being the youngest. Venus is the love Goddess of this land, and the most beautiful. Psyche's sisters and Venus are envious of Psyche. Venus is determined to prevent Psyche from stealing her title as the most beautiful. Psyche's sisters were already married by the time they reached, Psyche's age, causing the King and Queen to grow worried about Psyche's prospects for the future.

The Royal couple travel to consult the Oracle at Delphi to get a glimpse into Psyche's destiny...

In the inner depths of the temple, a virgin priestess inhales vapors and is seduced by prophetic voices. In a trance the priestess tells the King and Queen, "Dress Psyche for a wedding and for death, place her on top of a mountain, but she will not wed a mortal husband."

The tranquil breeze Zephyrus (God of the west wind), transports Psyche to the mountain. The mountain is the ascent to a mystical place, where spirit is present. Psyche crosses the threshold and goes into her castle made of gold. Will Psyche transform and meet her deepest most-profound eternal love, or will she die? What will be Psyche's destiny?

Every night on top of the mountain, a sweet spirit comes and visits Psyche. She senses it is her Divine counterpart, but she does not see his face.

One day, Psyche's sisters come to visit, and they demand to know what Psyche is doing on the mountain. They sense she is not telling them the truth, so they bully Psyche into doubting she will meet her true love and say, “The Oracle said, be prepared for death too.” The sisters give Psyche a lamp and a knife.

Psyche's sisters leave and now she is full of doubt. Psyche believes she will never have peace and live in joy. She is all alone with her lamp and decides to hide the knife under her pillow for protection. Zephyrus says to Psyche, [A woman is united with her Divine counterpart in the bridal chamber, and those united in the bridal chamber will not be separated. The mysteries of truth are made known in symbols and images. The bedchamber is hidden, and it is the center of the holy of the holies.] Psyche asks, do you mean sex?

No, no Zephyrus says, [the bedchamber is the sacred space deep in your mind, the center of the mystical eternal silence, where spiritual symbols and images reside.] Psyche says, "Oh, I do not understand. Zephyrus says, someday you will." The day has turned to darkness, and Psyche's love comes to visit, but she is not ready for her Divine supernal counterpart. She is full of self-doubt.

Psyche cannot receive the symbols of divine truth because she is not only doubtful, but she is not fully awakened to receive the fullness of her hidden connection with the Infinite. Therefore, she cannot connect with her Divine counterpart. As such, she cannot enter the holy of holies with him.

So, Psyche rises with her lamp in her left hand, and holds the knife in her right hand, ready to strike, but her love is startled and flies away…Psyche cries out to Zephyrus, what happened, why did he leave?

Zephyrus says, [at first, the curtain is hidden and that is how God manages creation, but when the curtain is torn and what inside appears, the building will be left deserted. And the whole godhead will flee from here, but not into the holy of holies, for it cannot mingle with pure light and perfect fullness.]

Venus hears about what had happened and is furious with Psyche. Eros, her son, is the spirit who visits Psyche every night. Self-doubt and psycho- spiritual ignorance must be overcome and transcended for Eros and Psyche to enter the bridal chamber.

Venus yells at Psyche, “You are not worthy of such an exalted bond of love with all your self-doubt and psycho- spiritual unawareness." Psyche pleads with Venus and says," Yes, I am worthy, and I want to understand my immortal nature." Venus says, “Ok” and she sends Psyche down into Hades, the underworld to remember her immortal nature and prove she is worthy.

While down in the depths, Psyche is given test after test to prove her worth. Psyche passes the tests with great fortitude, and as a result, she has died to her old self-doubting mortal ego self, and has transformed into the Goddess of the immortal soul, united with the Infinite.

Now she is worthy of Eros. Finally, she comes up from the underworld and emerges into the light of day.

Zephyrus greets Psyche and says, [the upper realm is opened for us in the lower realm, and that we might enter the hidden realm of truth. This is what is truly worthy and mighty, and we shall enter through symbols that are weak and insignificant. They are weak compared to perfect glory.

There is glory that surpasses glory, there is power that surpasses power. Perfect things have opened to us, the hidden things of truth. The holy of holies is revealed, and the bedchamber is its center.]

[Everyone who enters the bedchamber will kindle the light. If someone becomes an attendant of the bedchamber, that person will receive the light. If one does not receive it while here in this place, one cannot receive it in the other place.] Psyche, the main book of the Kabbalah -The Zohar, takes the verse 1:7 of the Song of Songs and gives us a gift. The ancient Kabbalists tell us the benefit of knowing our soul while here on earth. If we think it is unimportant to know our soul, we have to return again.

The Soul speaking to God in the Supernal world:

Tell me the mysteries of the supernal wisdom: How do you lead your flock in the upper world? Teach me some of the mysteries of the wisdom for I have not learned them. Teach me so I will not be in shame when I come among the eternal souls for until now, I have not reflected on the mysteries.

If you don't understand the beauty of the soul, if you return and haven't reflected in the wisdom before you came here and don't know anything of the mysteries of the upper world, you aren't merited to enter here. Therefore, return again. Learn those things that people consider to be unimportant and know the secrets of the upper world.

[Those who receive the light cannot be seen or grasped. Nothing can trouble such people even while they are living in this world. And when they leave this world, they have already received truth through images, and the world has become the eternal realm. To these people the eternal realm is fullness.

This is the way it is. It is revealed to such a person alone, hidden not in darkness and night but hidden in perfect day and holy light.]

Psyche says, thank you for your wisdom, Zephyrus. Before Zephyrus has a chance to answer, Zephyrus emerges over the mountains and Eros appears before Psyche's eyes.

Eros has also been given tests for his unworthiness, and lack of uniting with the Infinite too. He has transformed into a god; full of worldly- worthiness and spiritual fullness. He is the exalted god of mortal and immortality.

The tranquil serene breeze wraps Psyche with her deepest most- profound eternal love, Eros. Eros and Psyche woke up to their immortal nature and transcended their lower nature and united with the Infinite, and have proven, they are worthy of each other. They are ready to enter the holy of holies together, where the bedchamber becomes the bridal chamber.

The Bridal Chamber unites the masculine and feminine sides of the soul. She is her beloved's counterpart, and he is hers. I am my beloved's and my beloved is mine. The Divine Feminine is united with her Divine Masculine. Indeed, those who have united in the bridal chamber will no longer be separated.

Eros and Psyche have reunited after their long journey apart. Venus and Jupiter, (the king of the gods) bless them and say, “Congratulations, your union is rare! You have journeyed where few mortals travel, together you will ascend even further toward the Infinite of our entire universe both seen and unseen” …

Jupiter calls his messenger Mercury and tells him to gather everyone for the Mystical marriage. Jupiter also summons the god of wine, Dionysus. Dionysus says, “I want to be an intrinsic part of the celebration.”

For the last three years, I have been aging the Sangiovese grape in oak barrels. I will name the Sangiovese grape after you, Jupiter, and it will be forever known as the “Blood of Jupiter.” I will be honored to bring the delicious wine to the wedding.

Mercury gives Eros and Psyche his staff as a present and says … Congratulations, my Caduceus represents the foundation of a healthy relationship; Eros and Psyche you have earned the honor, and your wings.

Mercury gives "the eternal lovers" his caduceus. Eros and Psyche you have earned your wings. The caduceus is the equivalent to the Kundalini rising within the Chakra system of the east. Incidentally, this symbol is the medical sign. The two snakes of the caduceus and chakras represent the masculine and feminine energies, and as we transcend the polarities, we become centered and healthy- our human identity and our spiritual nature have merged and are one with the Infinite.

In the east, Krishna and Radha, Shiva and Shakti represent the equivalent to Eros and Psyche. Shiva and Shakti are depicted seated facing each other, in the Yab-Yum position. Eros and Psyche and Shiva and Shakti, and the devotion and spiritual love of Krishna and Radha are the supreme examples of mystical marriages. The sex between these couples' graduates as Tantric sex.

Jupiter says, "Eros and Psyche now that you have awakened to your immortal identity and reunited, you will live forever together!"

The Kabbalah teaches, their joining has long since taken place in the upper world. When the time comes for soul mates/twin flames to marry, the beloved force who knows each soul, rejoins them as they were at first and proclaims their union.

“Let there be spaces in your togetherness and let the winds of the heavens dance between you.”- Khalil Gibran.

Would you like to aspire to the mystical story of Eros and Psyche?

Are you ready to wake up to your Spiritual Superpower Point, and bring this awareness into a centered harmony?

Soul Mates/Twin Flames mirror their Divine nature; they do not own the mirror but regard the reflection with awe and devotion!

Time immemorial captivates the magic of Eros and Psyche! Their exalted bond of love is mesmerizing, as Eternity shines through time in their presence.

A divinely tranquil, gentle breeze flows over the mountains and wraps Psyche together with Eros. When you take a look at this painting, you know immediately that Psyche is totally fulfilled. She has been abducted by Eros, the ultimate spiritual connection. This abduction is not a negative, but a positive reaffirming of Eros's love for Psyche. They are a purely spiritual couple both wrapped in deep purple, symbolizing royalty. After their long, arduous time apart from one another, the twin souls are now reunited on earth. Clearly, they have never lost their heavenly bliss.

“Eros seizes and shakes my very soul, like the wind on the mountain shaking ancient oaks.”- Sappho.

Epilogue

A soul mate/twin flame is an extraordinary connection we have with another. What can we do to prepare ourselves for this amazing encounter?

"Your task is not to seek for love, but merely to seek and find all the barriers within yourself that you have built against it."-Rumi.

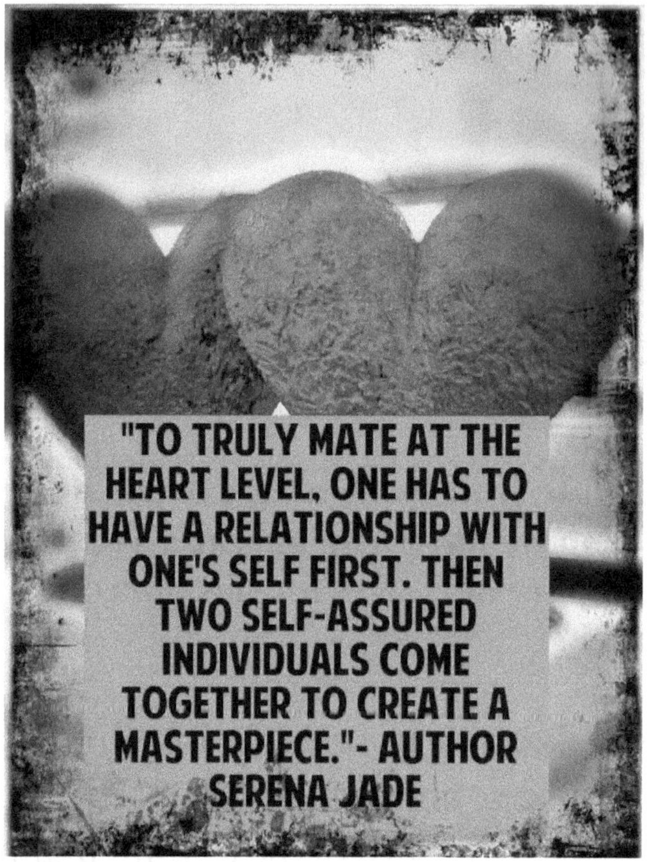

When we grow up in a flawed environment damage occurs to our sense of self. Understanding our role in our family structure enhances our ability to overcome defense mechanisms formed in early childhood. Making an **honest** study of our family and our role inside the system is the first step towards preparing for a soul mate/twin flame.

Devotion is defined in the dictionary as love, loyalty, or enthusiasm for a person, activity or cause. In this case, it's our love, loyalty and enthusiasm for our well-being. It's making a study of ourselves, and this will lead us to mastery of self.

When our heart is ready for intimacy - we have transcended our Co-Dependent and Dependent unhealthy defense mechanism.

What is Co-dependency?

It is well-known, the emotional and psychological unhealthy behavioral pattern: the co-dependent/dependent complex. The caretaker (i.e., co-dependent) feels responsible *for* the other person (i.e., the dependent). And being responsible *for* someone else breaks down a relationship and sets up a role that we play.

We live in this co-dependent/dependent society, as the dependent relies on the other person for their caretaking and is dependent on the other person for their emotional security. The co-dependent is the caretaker, but has not achieved true independence, and is also dependent on the other person to provide for their emotional security.

As we live in a co-dependent/dependent society, this creates the expectation that someone else needs to be responsible for another person. If one expects to be taken care of, and the other is responsible for them, we have an imbalance. However, if both people are responsible to themselves, we can honor the other person.

An example of a classic co-dependent and dependent relationship…

A woman doesn't have self-trust, so she has a reassurance behavioral pattern, where she seeks the man's approval. Now the man has the power to dictate her worth, based on his response. This translates to a needy dependent personality as opposed to being independent.

In an interdependent relationship both take care of each other, and are true lovers as opposed to the co-dependent and dependent! When we are responsible for ourselves, we want to take care of each other as opposed to what the other can do for me!

Usually, but not always it is the man responsible for his wife. This sets up a child to a parent relationship and as a result, we cannot honor the other person. The one who claims the role as a child is not seen as a separate person in the eyes of the one who assumes the parental role. In this child to a parent relationship, at least one of you, if not both, will be taken for granted. We now have a relationship, where we use one another for emotional security, sex, and money.

As the relationship is solidified as a child to the parent, one exudes dominance over the other person. When this imbalance of respect occurs within the unit, we have created a dominator and an accommodator. Neither person has achieved autonomy and therefore, cannot be independent. So, for that reason one does not respect the other and this creates mental put-downs which hurt and destroy the relationship.

In her book, The Heroine's Journey by Maureen Murdock, she explains: In patriarchal relationships, a dominant person and a submissive is the rule. The dominant person has to keep a one up position (abusing their power). To own one's power is to have full autonomy. If one had parents who put shame and doubt on them, then one does not own one's autonomy. One will get into ALL relationships, and role play the dominate person or submissive. To have self-knowledge is to know which one you are: Are you the dominant person or submissive?

"Where love reigns, there is no will to power; and where the will to power is paramount, love is lacking. The one is but the shadow of the other."- Carl Jung.

We are following a script written by society and hence, we are playing the lover as opposed to being a true intimate lover. Because our role cares about our survival, any chance of developing intimacy is destroyed. When we are aware of our unconscious survival needs, we will be able to see these needs are directing our emotions. True lovers exude independence, and do not have to control the other person with hurtful put-downs because they are not afraid of abandonment or engulfment.

What is abandonment and engulfment?

Abandonment and engulfment start when we are babies. Our caretakers are less than perfect people, and if they did not respond to our needs in a healthy way, we either respond as the seeker or sought. This is called Attachment theory in psychology.

The attachment experience understood by Freud but developed by psychologist John Bowlby, tells us we developed an anxious (seeker) or avoidant (sought) style of relating, based on the emotional availability of our caretakers.

Attachment is a deep and enduring emotional bond that connects one person to another across time and space (John Bowlby, 1969).

Abandonment and engulfment have its roots in attachment. In every relationship, whether it is with your spouse, parent, child, or friend. We have a pattern where one person is the anxious, seeker and the other, the avoidant, sought.

What is the seeker, anxious attachment style? The caretaker does not respond to the baby's cues and the baby can sense the coldness. When under stress this baby cries and is distressed but when and if the caretaker responds, the baby pushes the caretaker away. The baby does not feel safe and secure but feels abandoned.

When this baby grows up, they will focus their attention on their relationships, fearing the other person will abandon them. They will most likely become a pleaser because they fear being abandoned. They want togetherness and they focus their attention on the other person. But they still carry with them the response to push people away with how they communicate. Their response usually comes out in a demanding or angry way, further pushing the other person away. This scenario becomes a self-fulfilling prophecy from their fear of loss.

What is the avoidant, sought? This baby was less likely to cry when they were stressed and remain indifferent to their caretaker's response. This baby appeared to handle the stress with no outward appearance of distress. But when they took a closer look, their bodies underwent a lot of stress, but did not show it.

When this baby grows up, they will get into relationships and act as if they want to be left alone. Their fear is to surrender to someone else; they want their space. They usually focus on projects as opposed to their relationship. This becomes a self-fulfilling prophecy too, they will get their space, as they become more distant with their partners.

In the beginning of a relationship, both people are flowing and creating an unrealistic scenario as they give up all their time to be together. Down the road, we get complacent and start to take the other for granted. We start to separate and do not spend as much of our time together. The person who acts autonomous starts to pull away from the other. The person who is trying to avoid separation experiences the loss of all togetherness. Fear creates tension and the struggle for power and distance is upon us.

The ego hungers for wholeness, so we want to own the object of our love, as opposed to being identified with their traits.

Ideally, we need to switch from being the person who wants to be together, to the person who wants some space. This is not easy because switching brings up fear. The togetherness person fears loss and abandonment, thus cannot mentally detach from the other. They have a hard time being alone and seek the other, out of fear. The other feels smothered and conquered as if their space is being invaded. They feel left without their own identity and are afraid to be weakened by the other!

If we can switch back and forth, we create intimacy. The person who needs all togetherness can feel pursued when they stop abandoning themselves. The other, will want to be close when they have room to move!

The ultimate is when the togetherness person not only gives attention but receives the affection from the other; and the other not only receives warmth but also gives devotion. This is the moment of intimacy, when we give and receive from an emotional touch of the heart! Intimacy can only last a certain amount of time. For that reason, we need to be in touch with our own fear and know we are good enough to be emotionally close.

True lovers have transformed their abandonment and engulfment issues and are not identified with either the dependent or co-dependent.

Both people are two independent humans and become interdependent and take into consideration being in the other person's shoes. There is a sharing of empathy, as they are in tune with the other person's feelings and problems. The couple transforms into true lovers as opposed to acting the part of a lover!

How can we achieve true intimacy, and stop the unhealthy the co-dependent/ dependent relationship?

We must be responsible for ourselves, and this is not as simple as we may think. Being responsible for ourselves, but TO another and not FOR another is profound.

Being responsible for someone else is a role we play, as opposed to caring for someone as part of one's commitment.

Ideally, we need to be responsible for our own well-being, *feelings, actions, health*, money, shelter, food, clothes. Then, instead of outsourcing our feeling of being secure to others, we can internalize emotional security.

Once we are responsible for ourselves, we can honor others. We can share our body for sex as opposed to using another for one's own benefit. We also can share our resources with another, to enhance the relationship as opposed to using another for one's own allowance. However, to share we need to be able to share without losing our own power (independence).

When we have independence, interdependency is the ultimate destination.

What does interdependency look like?

Interdependency is when two people are autonomous, free from their family's and society's influence. They have emotional grounded stability and are independent. They do not need others to take care of their survival needs, nor do they feel the need to take care of others. However, they share their resources with one another, but do not lose their power to one another. They take responsibility for their feelings and actions. They honor space and togetherness and are honest with one another. They listen to each other without guilt, shame, or defensiveness. They are empathic towards one another and have high self-esteem. They are both emotionally committed to the relationship.

Are you up for the challenge?

The Vitruvian: a seamless blending of body, mind, and soul, embodying both the supernal and the earthly through the harmony of man and woman.

When the Body, Mind, Emotions and Soul come together…

The intellectual mind and our emotions influence our decisions. Our mind thinks one way, but our emotions say something quite different. We do not **feel** good enough, so we make unhealthy choices.

However, when our mind and emotions are on the same team, we have the understanding within to make a smart decision. The sharp effectiveness in all areas of life is laying the groundwork towards welcoming a soul mate/twin flame into our arms.

Our body is a gift, and we need to **feel** thankful that we have one. Taking good proper care of our valuable present is another step towards preparing to meet one's soul mate/twin flame. The impact our emotions have on us is powerful. How we feel about ourselves is paramount, and we will overeat if we do not feel worthy enough. Most people **think** about exercising, instead of acting upon it. When the union of our mind and emotions come together, we are empowered to get up and start moving!

We now have a sense of our whole self and can appreciate our world and other cultures. We have an open mind and can comprehend all countries and continents are interconnected by the same cosmic force.

The breakthrough is to know that reuniting with our spiritual loved ones is a gift.

By meeting our soul's mates/twin flame, we are no longer thinking just about our own needs. We are coming together for an impressively immense worldly and spiritual purpose!

Do you want to be exalted lovers like Eros and Psyche?

What are your stumbling blocks that are preventing you from manifesting an exalted love connection?

Do you believe you have barriers?

Or do you think other people have obstacles?

Aspire to the mystical love story of Eros and Psyche!

Questions To Ask Yourself:

Are you aware the knowledge of soul mates and twin flames are revealed through the esoteric wisdom of all the major religions past and present?

Where did you first hear about twin flames?

Why do you feel you met your soul's counterpart?

Do you know the difference between your ego and soul?

Are you in touch with your soul's passion and purpose?

Do you know all your shadow material?

The shadow coined by Carl Jung are psychological material we are not identified with, and gets stored in our unconscious, out of sight from us, but projected onto others.

The Shadow: "The thing a person has no wish to be." – Carl Jung

Are you aware of your masculine and feminine qualities within yourself?—And have Transcended them?

Do you understand you need to make the union with your own soul and ego, known as the mystical marriage?

Twin Flames are mirrors to their Supernal nature. Do you know where your Bindu is? And what it stands for?

Did you transcend a traditional relationship? Because that is what we have inherited.

If you have transcended a traditional relationship, only then can you be with a mirror image of your Supernal nature!!

Did you transcend your survival needs? - Being responsible for managing your life?

Are you the dominant person, does your behavior convey-the all-important, all-powerful, all-knowing, or are you submissive- controlled by, or influenced by, or rely too heavily on someone else?

Did you make your karma (obstacles) right?

Are you on the social path or inward path?

About the Author

וְהֹו

Serena Jade

She Teaches What She Lives: Raising The Sparks Through Body, Mind, & Soul...

Serena Jade is a modern mystic of the body, mind, and soul- a woman who embodies the wisdom she teaches. A psycho-spiritual author, and globe-trotting yoga teacher who blends Freudian/Jungian unconscious dives with a passion for uncovering the mystical origins of soul mates and twin flames. She weaves a mystical & scientific tapestry of Tantra, Sufi, Gnostic, Kabbalah as well as Philosophy of Physics into her repertoire.

She is the author of several books including: Charismatic Connection: Whispers of A Love That Transcends Time. Her works are mainly focused on psychology, religion, and travel. She draws inspiration from Ancient and Modern Mysticism, Joseph Campbell, and Carl Jung. Serena Jade's books, retreats, courses, yoga classes, and coaching are built around the idea of living life exuding wellness and following one's own soul's passion and purpose.

Teaching: As a certified Kundalini Tantra Yoga Instructor, Serena Jade imparts wisdom on raising divine energy and uplifting the body and mind. Her teachings blend laughter, sound healing meditation, restorative, and spiritual practices.

Wellness Advocate: Serena Jade's journey extends beyond books and teachings. She inspires people to explore the world, cultivate physical fitness, balance the mind, and awaken their sixth sense.

Unparalleled Wisdom: Her travels, knowledge, and insight into the highest spiritual attainment make her a beacon of light for those seeking inner transformation.

To know more about Serena Jade, visit her website at SerenaJade.co or her company, The House of Raising The Sparks, TheHouseofRaisingTheSparks.com.

Endnotes

Carl Jung, AION, Paragraph 347, Page 222

Joseph Dan, The Early Kabbalah

Rabbi Adin Steinsaltz, The Soul

Daniel Matt, God & The Big Bang

Gershom Scholem, Major Trends In Jewish Mysticism, Schocken Publishing, 1995

Maureen Murdock, The Heroine's Journey: Woman's Quest for Wholeness, Massachusetts: Shambhala Publications, 1990.

UnlimitedSecrets-Chabad.org

Translation of the Gates of Reincarnation, Rabbi Luria, 2015

Carl Jung, Collected Works, Volume 7, Par.32

Sofia A. Souli, The Love Life of the Ancient Greeks, Michalis Toubis, 1997

Gospel of Philip, Nag Hammadi Library

Kevin Todeschi, Edgar Cayce on Soul Mates, A.R.E. Press, 1999

Patricia Joudry, Maurie Pressman, M.D., Twin Souls; A Guide to Finding Your True Spiritual Partner, Carol Southern Books, an imprint of Crown Publishers Inc., 1995-

The Sufis by Idries Shah

Omraam Mikhael Aivanhov, Love and Sexuality, Prosveta Ltd.1976

Michael, Finding Your Soul Mate, Samuel Weiser, Inc., 1992

Rabbi Philip Berg, Kabbalah for the Layman, Kabbalah Publishing, 1993

On The Origin of The World, Gnostic Manuscript

Rabbi Philip Berg, Wheels of a Soul, Kabbalah Publishing, 2005

Rabbi Philip Berg, To The Power of One, Kabbalah Publishing, 1991

Llewellyn Vaughan-Lee "A Dangerous Love"-
https://youtu.be/Q7pe_GLp_6o?si=XnJg3RHkxtf6lPB2

Yedid Nefesh, Chabad.org

www.ingramcontent.com/pod-product-compliance
Lightning Source LLC
LaVergne TN
LVHW060042210926
848481LV00013B/3935